St. Ambrose
The Book Concerning Widows

St. Ambrose
The Book Concerning Widows

St. Ambrose
The Book Concerning Widows

© Lighthouse Publishing 2018

All rights reserved. Without limiting the rights under copyright reserved above, no part of this publication may be reproduced, stored in a retrieval system, or transmitted, in any form or by any means (electronic, mechanical, photocopying, recording or otherwise), without the prior written permission of the copyright owner of this book.

Published by
Lighthouse Christian Publishing
SAN 257-4330
5531 Dufferin Drive
Savage, Minnesota, 55378
United States of America

www.lighthousechristianpublishing.com

The Book Concerning Widows.

Introduction

THE writer informs us himself at the beginning of his treatise that he felt moved by the example of St. Paul, after speaking about virgins, to continue with the subject of widows. But there was also another matter in his own diocese which touched him personally, and caused him at once to take up the matter. A certain widow who had several daughters, some married already and others of marriageable age, began to think of a second marriage for herself. St. Ambrose, partly for her own sake, partly that it might not be supposed that he had in any way advised the step, published the following treatise.

In the first place he affirms that the profession of widowhood comes very close to that of virginity, and is to be esteemed far above the married state. He proves this by the testimony of St. Paul and by his description of one who is a widow indeed; also by many examples taken both from the old and New Testament. Having mentioned St. Peter's wife's mother, he turns more particularly to the widow for whose sake he is writing, though he avoids mentioning her name, pointing out how really empty and insufficient are all the reasons she is setting before herself for marrying again. The marriage bond is, indeed, he says, holy and good, and the married and single are as various kinds of flowers in the field of the church. There is, however, more corn produced than lilies, more that is married than virgin. He points out that widowhood has been held in dishonor by idolaters alone, for which reason it may well be held in honor by Christians. St. Ambrose does not condemn a second marriage, though placing widowhood before it, as being bound to aim at leading those committed to his loving care to the highest possible degree of perfection. The treatise was written not long after that concerning Virgins, that is, soon after A.D. 377.

THE BOOK CONCERNING WIDOWS
CHAPTER I.

After having written about virgins, it seemed needful to say something concerning widows, since the Apostle joins the two classes together, and the latter are as it were teachers of the former, and far superior to those who are married. Elijah was sent to a widow, a great mark of honor; yet widows are not honorable like her of Sarepta, unless they copy her virtues, notably hospitality. The avarice of men is rebuked, who forfeit the promises of God by their grasping.

1. S<small>INCE</small> I have treated of the honor of virgins in three books, it is fitting now, my brethren, that a treatise concerning widows should come in order; for I ought not to leave them without honor, nor to separate them from the commendation belonging to virgins, since the voice of the Apostle has joined them to virgins, according to what is written: "The unmarried woman and the virgin careth for the things of the Lord, that she may be holy both in body and in spirit." For in a certain manner the inculcation of virginity is strengthened by the example of widows. They who have preserved their marriage bed undefiled are a testimony to virgins that chastity is to be preserved for God. And it is almost a mark of no less virtue to abstain from marriage, which was once a delight, than to remain ignorant of the pleasures of wedlock. They are strong in each point, in that they regret not wedlock, the faith of which they keep, and entangle not themselves with wedded pleasures, lest they appear weak and not able to take care of themselves.

2. But in this particular virtue is contained also the prizes of liberty. For: "The wife is bound as long as her husband

liveth; but if her husband fall asleep she is freed: let her marry whom she will, only in the Lord. But she will be happier if she so abide, after my judgment, for I think I also have the Spirit of God." Evidently, then, the Apostle has expressed the difference, having said that the one is bound, and stated that the other is happier, and that he asserts not so much as the result of his own judgment, as of the infusion of the Spirit of God; that the decision should be seen to be heavenly, not human.

3. And what is the teaching of the fact that at that time when the whole human race was afflicted by famine and Elias was sent to the widow? And see how for each is reserved her own special grace. An angel is sent to the Virgin, a prophet to the widow. Notice, farther, that in one case it is Gabriel, in the other Elisha. The most excellent chiefs of the number of angels and prophets are seen to be chosen. But there is no praise simply in widowhood, unless there be added the virtues of widowhood. For, indeed, there were many widows, but one is preferred to all, in which fact it is not so much that others are called back from their pursuit as that they are stimulated by the example of virtue.

4. What is said at first makes the ears attentive, although the simplicity itself of the understanding has weight to attract widows to the pattern of virtue; since each seems to excel, not according to her profession, but her merit, and the grace of hospitality is not lost sight of by God, Who, as He Himself related in the Gospel, rewards a cup of cold water with the exceeding recompense of eternity, and compensates the small measure of meal and oil by an unfailing abundance of plenty ever coming in. For if one

of the heathen has said that all the possessions of friends should be common, how much more ought those of relatives to be common! For we are relatives who are bound into one body.

5. But we are not bound by any prescribed limit of hospitality. For why do you think that what is of this world is private property when this world is common? Or why do you consider the fruits of the earth are private, when the earth itself is common property? "Behold," He said, "the fowls of the air, they sow not, neither do they reap." For to those to whom nothing is private property nothing is wanting, and God, the master of His own word, knows how to keep His promise. Again, the birds do not gather together, and yet they eat, for our heavenly Father feeds them. But we turning aside the warnings of a general utterance to our private advantage, God says: "Every tree which has in it the fruit of a tree yielding seed shall be to you for meat, and to every beast, and to every bird, and to everything that creepeth upon the earth." By gathering together we come to want, and by gathering together we are made empty. For we cannot hope for the promise, who keep not the saying. It is also good for us to attend to the precept of hospitality, to be ready to give to strangers, for we, too, are strangers in the world.

6. But how holy was that widow, who, when pinched by extreme hunger, observed the reverence due to God, and was not using the food for herself alone, but was dividing it with her son, that she might not outlive her dear offspring. Great is the duty of affection, but that of religion brings more return. For as no one ought to be set before her son, so the prophet of God ought to be set

before her son and her preservation. For she is to be believed to have given to him not a little food, but the whole support of her life, who left nothing for herself. So hospitable was she that she gave the whole, so full of faith that she believed at once.

CHAPTER II.

The precepts of the Apostle concerning a widow indeed are laid down, such as, that she bring up children, attend to her parents, desire to please God, show herself irreproachable, set forth a ripeness of merits, have been the wife of one man. St. Ambrose notes, however, that a second marriage was not condemned by St. Paul, and adds that widows must have a good report for virtue with all. The reasons why younger widows are to be avoided, and what is meant by its being better to marry than to burn. St. Ambrose then goes on to speak of the dignity of widows, shown by the fact that any injury done to them is visited by the anger of God.

7. So, then, a widow is not only marked off by bodily abstinence, but is distinguished by virtue, to whom I do not give commandments, but the Apostle. I am not the only person to do them honor, but the Doctor of the Gentiles did so first, when he said: "Honor widows that are widows indeed. But if any widow have children or nephews, let her first learn to govern her own house, and to requite her parents." Whence we observe that each inclination of affection ought to exist in a widow, to love her children and to do her duty to her parents. So when discharging her duty to her parents she is teaching her children, and is rewarded herself by her own compliance with duty, in that what she performs for others benefits herself.

8. "For this," says he, "is acceptable with God." So that if thou, O widow, carest for the things of God, thou oughtest to follow after that which thou hast learnt to be well pleasing to God. And, indeed, the Apostle somewhat farther back, exhorting widows to the pursuit of continence, said that they mind the things of the Lord. But elsewhere, when a widow who is approved is to be

selected, she is bidden not only to bear in mind but also to hope in the Lord: "For she that is a widow indeed," it is said, "and desolate, must hope in God, and be instant in supplications and prayers night and day." And not without reason does he show that these ought to be blameless, to whom, as virtuous works are enjoined, so, too, great respect is paid, so that they are honored even by bishops.

9. And of what kind she ought to be who is chosen the description is given in the words of the teacher himself: "Not less than threescore years old, having been the wife of one man." Not that old age alone makes the widow, but that the merits of the widow are the duties of old age. For she certainly is the more noble who represses the heat of youth, and the impetuous ardor of youthful age, desiring neither the tenderness of a husband, nor the abundant delights of children, rather than one who, now worn out in body, cold in age, of ripe years, can neither grow warm with pleasures, nor hope for offspring.

10. Nor in truth is any one excluded from the devotion of widowhood, if after entering upon a second marriage, which the precepts of the Apostle certainly do not condemn as though the fruit of chastity were lost, if she be again loosed from her husband. She will have, indeed, the merit of her chastity, even if it be tardy, but she will be more approved who has tried a second marriage, for the desire of chastity is conspicuous in her, for the other old age or shame seems to have put an end to marrying.

11. Nor yet is bodily chastity alone the strong purpose of the widow, but a large and most abundant exercise of virtue. "Well reported of for good works, if she have

brought up children; if she have lodged strangers; if she have washed the saints' feet; if she have ministered to those suffering tribulation; if, lastly, she have followed after every good work." You see how many practices of virtue he has included. He demands, first of all, the duty of piety; secondly, the practice of hospitality and humble service; thirdly, the ministry of mercy and liberality in assisting; and, lastly, the performance of every good work.

12. And he, therefore, that the younger should be avoided, because they are not able to fulfill the requirements of so high a degree of virtue. For youth is prone to fall because the heat of various desires is inflamed by the warmth of glowing youth, and it is the part of a good doctor to keep off the materials of sin. For the first exercise in training the soul is to turn away sin, the second to implant virtue. Yet, since the Apostle knew that Anna, the widow of fourscore years, from her youth was a herald of the works of the Lord, I do not think that he thought that the younger should be excluded from the devotion of widowhood, especially as he said: "It is better to marry than to burn." For certainly he recommended marriage as a remedy, that she who would else perish might be saved; he did not prescribe the choice that one who could contain should not follow chastity, for it is one thing to succor one who is falling, another to persuade to virtue.

13. And what shall I say of human judgments, since in the judgments of God the Jews are set forth as having offended the Lord in nothing more than violating what was due to the widow and the rights of minors? This is proclaimed by the voices of the prophets as the cause

which brought upon the Jews the penalty of rejection. This is mentioned as the only cause which will mitigate the wrath of God against their sin, if they honor the widow, and execute true judgment for minors, for thus we read: "Judge the fatherless, deal justly with the widow, and come let us reason together, saith the Lord." And elsewhere: "The Lord shall maintain the orphan and the widow." And again: "I will abundantly bless her widow." Wherein also the likeness of the Church is foreshadowed. You see, then, holy widows, that that office which is honored by the assistance of divine grace must not be degraded by impure desire.

CHAPTER III.

St. Ambrose returns to the story of the widow of Sarepta, and shows that she represented the Church, hence that she was an example to virgins, married women, and widows. Then he refers to theprophet as setting forth Christ, inasmuch as he foretold the mysteries and the rain which was to come. Next he touches upon and explains the twofold sign of Gideon, and points out that it is not in every one's power to work miracles, and that the Incarnation of Christ and the rejection of the Jews were foreshadowed in that account.

14. To return to what was treated of above, what is the meaning of the fact that when there was a very great famine in all the land, yet the care of God was not wanting to the widow, and the prophet was sent to sustain her? And when in this story the Lord warns me that He is about to speak in truth, He seems to bid my ears attend to a mystery. For what can be more true than the mystery of Christ and the Church? Not, then, without a purpose is one preferred amongst many widows. Who is such a one, to whom so great a prophet who was carried up into heaven, should be guided, especially at that time when the heaven was shut for three years and six months, when there was a great famine in the whole land? The famine was everywhere, and yet notwithstanding this widow did not want. What are these three years? Are they not, perchance, those in which the Lord came to the earth and could not find fruit on the fig-tree, according to that which is written: "Behold, there are three years that I came seeking fruit on this fig-tree, and find none."

15. This is assuredly that widow of whom it was said: "Rejoice, thou barren that bearest not, break forth and cry, thou that availest not with child; for many are the children

of the desolate, more than of her who hath a husband." And well is she a widow of whom it is well said: "Thou shalt not remember thy shame and thy widowhood, for I am the Lord Who make thee." And perchance therefore is she a widow who has lost her Husband indeed in the suffering of His body, but in the day of judgment shall receive again the Son of Man Whom she seemed to have lost. "For a short time have I forsaken thee," He says, in order that, being forsaken, she may the more gloriously keep her faith.

16. All, then, have an example to imitate, virgins, married women, and widows. And perchance is the Church therefore a virgin, married, and a widow, because they are one body in Christ. She is then that widow for Whose sake when there was a dearth of the heavenly Word on earth, the prophets were appointed, for there was a widow who was barren, yet reserved her bringing forth for its own time.

17. So that his person does not seem to us of small account, who by his word moistened the dry earth with the dew of heaven, and unlocked the closed heavens certainly not by human power. For who is he who can open the heavens except Christ, for Whom daily out of sinners' food is gathered, an increase for the Church? For it is not in the power of man to say: "The barrel of meal shall not waste, and the cruse of oil shall not fail, until the day on which the Lord shall send rain on the earth." For though it be the rule of the prophets to speak thus, the voice is in truth that of the Lord. And so it is stated first: "For thus saith the Lord." For it is of the Lord to vouch for a continuance of heavenly sacraments, and to promise that

the grace of spiritual joy shall not fail, to grant the defenses of life, the seals of faith, the gifts of virtues.

18. But what does this mean: "Until the day on which the Lord shall send rain on the earth"? except that He, too, "shall come down like rain upon a fleece, and like the drops that water the earth." In which passage is disclosed the mystery of the old history where Gideon, the warrior of the mystic conflict, receiving the pledge of future victory, recognized the spiritual sacrament in the vision of his mind, that that rain was the dew of the Divine Word, which first came down on the fleece, when all the earth was parched with continual drought, and by a second true sign, moistened the floor of all the earth with a shower, whilst dryness was upon the fleece.

19. For the prescient man observed the sign of the future growth of the Church. For first in Judæa the dew of the divine utterance began to give moisture (for "in Jewry is God known"), whilst the whole earth remained without the dew of faith. But when Joseph's flock began to deny God, and by venturing on various enormous offences to incur guilt before God, then when the dew of the heavenly shower was poured on the whole earth, the people of the Jews began to grow dry and parched in their own unbelief, when the clouds of prophecy and the healthful shower of the Apostles watered the holy Church gathered together from all parts of the world. This is that rain, now condensed from earthly moisture, now from mountain mists, but diffused throughout the whole world in the salutary shower of the heavenly Scriptures.

20. By this example, then, it is shown that not all can merit the miracles of divine power, but they who are aided by the pursuits of religious devotion, and that they lose the fruits of divine working who are devoid of reverence for heaven. It is also shown in a mystery that the Son of God, in order to restore the Church, took upon Himself the mystery of a human body, casting off the Jewish people, from whom the counselor and the prophet and the miracles of the divine benefits were taken away, because that as it were by a kind of national blemish they were not willing to believe in the Son of God.

CHAPTER IV.

By the example of Anna St. Ambrose shows what ought to be the life of widows, and shows that she was an example of chastity at every age. From this he argues that there are three degrees of the same virtue, all of which are included in the Church, and sets forth several examples in Mary, in Anna, and in Susanna. But, he adds, the state of virginity is superior to either of the others, but that a widow ought to take greater care for the preservation of her good name.

21. SCRIPTURE then teaches as how much grace is conferred by unity, and how great is the gift of divine blessing in widows. And since such honor is given them by God, we must observe what mode of life corresponds thereto; for Anna shows what widows ought to be, who, left destitute by the early death of her husband, yet obtained the reward of full praise, being intent not less on the duties of religion than on the pursuit of chastity. A widow, it is said, of fourscore and four years, a widow who departed not from the temple, a widow who served God night and day with fastings and with prayers.

22. You see what sort of person a widow is said to be, the wife of one man, tested also by the progress of age, vigorous in religion, and worn out in body, whose resting-place is the temple, whose conversation is prayer, whose life is fasting, who in the times of day and night by a service of unwearied devotion, though the body acknowledge old age, yet knows no age in her piety. Thus is a widow trained from her youth, thus is she spoken of in her age, who has kept her widowhood not through the chance of time, nor through weakness of body, but by large-heartedness in virtue. For when it is said that she was for seven years from her virginity with her husband,

it is a setting forth that the things which are the support of her old age began in the aims of her youth.

23. And so we are taught that the virtue of chastity is threefold, one kind that of married life, a second that of widowhood, and the third that of virginity, for we do not so set forth one as to exclude others. These result each in that which belongs to each. The training of the Church is rich in this, that it has those whom it may set before others, but has none whom it rejects, and would that it never could have any! We have so spoken of virginity as not to reject widowhood, we so reverence widows as to reserve its own honor for wedlock. It is not our precepts but the divine sayings which teach this.

24. Let us remember then how Mary, how Anna, and how Susanna are spoken of. But since not only must we celebrate their praises but also follow their manner of life, let us remember where Susanna, and Anna, and Mary are found, and observe how each is spoken of with her special commendation, and where each is mentioned, she that is married in the garden, the widow in the temple, the virgin in her secret chamber.

25. But in the former the fruit is later, in virginity it is earlier; old age proves them, virginity is the praise of youth, and does not need the help of years, being the fruit of every age. It becomes early years, it adorns youth, it adds to the dignity of age, and at all ages it has the gray hairs of its righteousness, the ripeness of its gravity, the veil of modesty, which does hinder devotion and increases religion. For we see by what follows that holy Mary went every year with Joseph to Jerusalem on the

solemn day of the Passover. Everywhere in company with the Virgin is eager devotion and a zealous sharer of her chastity. Nor is the Mother of the Lord puffed up, as though secure of her own merits, but the more she recognized her merit, the more fully did she pay her vows, the more abundantly did she perform her service, the more fully did she discharge her office, the more religiously did she perform her duty and fill up the mystic time.

26. How much more then does it beseem you to be intent on the pursuit of chastity, lest you leave any place for unfavorable opinion who have the evidence of your modesty and your behavior alone. For a virgin, though in her also character rather than the body has the first claim, puts away calumny by the integrity of her body, a widow who has lost the assistance of being able to prove her virginity undergoes the inquiry as to her chastity not according to the word of a midwife, but according to her own manner of life. Scripture, then, has shown how attentive and religious should be the disposition of a widow.

CHAPTER V.

Liberality to the poor is recommended by the example of the widow the Gospel, whose two mites were preferred to the large gifts of the rich. The two mites are treated as mystically representing the two Testaments. What that treasure is for which we are taught to offer, after the example of the wise men, three gifts, or after that of the widow, two. St. Ambrose concludes the chapter by an exhortation to widows to be zealous in good works.

27. IN the same book, too, but in another place, we are taught how fitting it is to be merciful and liberal towards the poor, and that this feeling should not be checked by the consideration of our poverty, since liberality is determined not by the amount of our possessions, but by the disposition of giving. For by the voice of the Lord that widow is preferred to all of whom it was said: "This widow hath cast in more than all." In which instance the Lord characteristically teaches all, that none should be held back from giving assistance through shame at his own poverty, and that the rich should not flatter themselves that they seem to give more than the poor. For the piece of money out of a small stock is richer than treasures out of abundance, because it is not the amount that is given but the amount that remains which is considered. No one gives more than she who has left nothing for herself.

28. Why do you, rich woman, boast yourself by comparison with the poor, and when you are all loaded with gold, and drag along the ground a costly robe, desire to be honored as though she were inferior and small in comparison with your riches, because you have surpassed the needy with your gifts? Rivers too overflow, when they are too full, but a draught from a brook is more pleasant.

New wine foams while fermenting, and the husbandman does not consider as lost that which runs over. While the harvest is being threshed out, grains of corn fall from the groaning floor; but though the harvests fail, the barrel of meal wastes not, and the cruse full of oil gives forth. But the draught emptied the casks of the rich, while the tiny cruse of oil of the widow gave abundance. That, then, is to be reckoned which you give for devotion, not what you cast forth disdainfully. For in fine, no one gave more than she who fed the prophet with her children's nourishment. And so since no one gave more, no one had greater merit. This has a moral application.

29. And considering the mystical sense, one must not despise this woman casting in two mites into the treasury. Plainly the woman was noble who in the divine judgment was found worthy to be preferred to all. Perchance it is she who of her faith has given two testaments for the help of man, and so no one has done more. Nor could anyone equal the amount of her gift, who joined faith with mercy. Do you, then, whoever you are, who exercise your life the practice of widowhood, not hesitate to cast into the treasury the two mites, full of faith and grace.

30. Happy is she who out of her treasure brings forth the perfect image of the King. Your treasure is wisdom, your treasure is chastity and righteousness, your treasure is a good understanding, such as was that treasure from which the Magi, when they worshipped the Lord, brought forth gold, frankincense, and myrrh; setting forth by gold the power of a king, venerating God by the frankincense, and by myrrh acknowledging the resurrection of the body. You too have this treasure if you look into yourself: "For

we have this treasure in earthen vessels." You have gold which you can give, for God does not exact of you the precious gift of shining metal, but that gold which at the day of judgment the fire shall be unable to consume. Nor does He require precious gifts, but the good odor of faith, which the altars of your heart send forth and the disposition of a religious mind exhales.

31. From this treasure, then, not only the three gifts of the Magi but also the two mites of the widow are taken, on which the perfect image of the heavenly King shines forth, the brightness of His glory and the image of His substance. Precious, too, are those hardly earned gains of chastity which the widow gives of her labor and daily task, continually night and day working at her task, and by the wakeful labor of her profitable chastity gathering treasure; that she may preserve the couch of her deceased husband unviolated, be able to support her dear children, and to minister to the poor. She is to be preferred to the rich, she it is who shall not fear the judgment of Christ.

32. Strive to equal her, my daughters: "It is good to be zealously affected in a good thing." "Covet earnestly the best gifts." The Lord is ever looking upon you, Jesus looks upon you when He goes to the treasury, and you think that of the gain of your good works assistance is to be given to those in need. What is it, then, that you should give your two mites and gain in return the Lord's Body? Go not, then, empty into the sight of the Lord your God, empty of mercy, empty of faith, empty of chastity; for the Lord Jesus is wont to look upon and to commend not the empty, but those who are rich in virtues. Let the maiden see you at work, let her see you ministering to others. For

this is the return which you owe to God, that you should make your return to God from the progress of others. No return is more acceptable to God than the offerings of piety.

CHAPTER VI.

Naomi is an instance of a widow receiving back from her daughter-in-law the fruits of her own good training, and is a token that necessary support will never fail the good widow. And if her life appears sad, she is happy, since the promises of the Lord are made to her. St. Ambrose then touches upon the benefits of weeping.

33. DOES the widow Naomi seem to you of small account, who supported her widowhood on the gleanings from another's harvest, and who, when heavy with age, was supported by her daughter-in-law? It is a great benefit both for the support and for the advantage of widows, that they so train their daughters-in-law as to have in them a support in full old age, and, as it were, payment for their teaching and reward for their training. For to her who has well taught and well instructed her daughter-in-law a Ruth will never be wanting who will prefer the widowed life of her mother-in-law to her father's house, and if her husband also be dead, will not leave her, will support her in need, comfort her in sorrow, and not leave her if sent away; for good instruction will never know want. So that Naomi, deprived of her husband and her two sons, having lost the offspring of her fruitfulness, lost not the reward of her pious care, for she found both a comfort in sorrow and a support in poverty.

34. You see, then, holy women, how fruitful a widow is in the offspring of virtues, and the results of her own merits, which cannot come to an end. A good widow, then, knows no want, and if she be weary through age, in extreme poverty, yet she has as a rule the reward of the training she has given. Though the nearest to herself have failed, she finds those not so near akin to cherish their

mother, revere their parent, and by the trifling gifts for her support desire to gain the fruit of their own kindness, for richly are gifts to a widow repaid. She asks food and pays back treasures.

35. But she seems to spend sad days, and to pass her time in tears. And she is the more blessed in this, for by a little weeping she purchases for herself everlasting joys, and at the cost of a few moments gains eternity. To such it is well said: "Blessed are ye that weep, for ye shall laugh." Who then would prefer the deceitful appearances of present joys to the pleasure of future freedom from anxiety? Does he seem to us an insignificant authority, the elect forefather of the Lord after the flesh, who ate ashes as it were bread, and mingled his drink with weeping, and by his tears at night gained for himself the joy of redemption in the morning? Whence did he gain that great joy except that he greatly wept, and, as it were, at the price of his tears obtained the grace of future glory for himself.

36. The widow has, then, this excellent recommendation, that while she mourns her husband she also weeps for the world, and the redeeming tears are ready, which shed for the dead will benefit the living. The weeping of the eyes is fitted to the sadness of the mind, it arouses pity, lessens labor, relieves grief, and preserves modesty, and she no longer seems to herself so wretched, finding comfort in tears which are the pay of love and proofs of pious memory.

CHAPTER VII.

By the example of Judith is shown that courage is not wanting in widows; her preparation for her visit to Holofernes is dwelt upon, as also her chastity and her wisdom, her sobriety and moderation. Lastly, St. Ambrose, after demonstrating that she was no less brave than prudent, sets forth her modesty after her success.

37. BUT bravery also is usually not wanting to a good widow. For this is true bravery, which surpasses the usual nature and the weakness of the sex by the devotion of the mind, such as was in her who was named Judith, who of herself alone was able to rouse up from utter prostration and defend from the enemy men broken down by the siege, smitten with fear, and pining with hunger. For she, as we read, when Holofernes, dreaded after his success in so many battles, had driven countless thousands of men within the walls; when the armed men were afraid, and were already treating about the final surrender, went forth outside the wall, both excelling that army which she delivered, and braver than that which she put to flight.

38. But in order to learn the dispositions of ripe widowhood, run through the course of the Scriptures. From the time when her husband died she laid aside the garments of mirth, and took those of mourning. Every day she was intent on fasting except on the Sabbath and the Lord's Day and the times of holy days, not as yielding to desire of refreshment, but out of respect for religion. For this is that which is said: "Whether ye eat or drink, all is to be done in the name of Jesus Christ," that even the very refreshment of the body is to have respect to the worship of holy religion. So then, holy Judith, strengthened by lengthened mourning and by daily fasting, sought not the

enjoyments of the world regardless of danger, and strong in her contempt for death. In order to accomplish her stratagem she put on that robe of mirth, wherewith in her husband's lifetime she was wont to be clothed, as though she would give pleasure to her husband, if she freed her country. But she saw another man whom she was seeking to please, even Him, of Whom it is said: "After me cometh a Man Who is preferred before me." And she did well in resuming her bridal ornaments when about to fight, for the reminders of wedlock are the arms of chastity, and in no other way could a widow please or gain the victory.

39. Why relate the sequel? How she amongst thousands of enemies, remained chaste. Why speak of her wisdom, in that she designed such a scheme? She chose out the commander, to ward off from herself the insolence of inferiors, and prepare an opportunity for victory. She reserved the merit of abstinence and the grace of chastity. For unpolluted, as we read, either by food or by adultery, she gained no less a triumph over the enemy by preserving her chastity than by delivering her country.

40. What shall I say of her sobriety? Temperance, indeed, is the virtue of women. When the men were intoxicated with wine and buried in sleep, the widow took the sword, put forth her hand, cut off the warrior's head, and passed unharmed through the midst of the ranks of the enemy. You notice, then, how much drunkenness can injure a woman, seeing that wine so weakens men that they are overcome by women. Let a widow, then, be temperate, pure in the first place from wine, that she may be pure from adultery. He will tempt you in vain, if wine tempts

you not. For if Judith had drunk she would have slept with the adulterer. But because she drank not, the sobriety of one without difficulty was able both to overcome and to escape from a drunken army.

41. And this was not so much a work of her hands, as much more a trophy of her wisdom. For having overcome Holofernes by her hand alone, she overcame the whole army of the enemies by her wisdom. For hanging up the head of Holofernes, a deed which the wisdom of the men had been unable to plan, she raised the courage of her countrymen, and broke down that of the enemy. She stirred up her own friends by her modesty, and struck terror into the enemy so that they were put to flight and slain. And so the temperance and sobriety of one widow not only subdued her own nature, but, which is far more, even made men more brave.

42. And yet she was not so elated by this success, though she might well rejoice and exult by right of her victory, as to give up the exercises of her widowhood, but refusing all who desired to wed her she laid aside her garments of mirth and took again those of her widowhood, not caring for the adornments of her triumph, thinking those things better whereby vices of the body are subdued than those whereby the weapons of an enemy are overcome.

CHAPTER VIII.

Though many other widows came near to Judith in virtue, St. Ambrose proposes to speak of Deborah only. What a pattern of virtue she must have been for widows, who was chosen to govern and defend men. It was no small glory to her that when her son was over the host he refused to go forth to battle unless she would go also. So that she led the army and foretold the result. In this story the conflicts and triumphs of the Church, and her spiritual weapons, are set forth, and every excuse of weakness is taken from women.

43. AND in order that it may not seem as if only one widow had fulfilled this inimitable work, it seems in no way doubtful that there were many others of equal or almost equal virtue, for good seed corn usually bears many ears filled with grains. Doubt not, then, that that ancient seed-time was fruitful in the characters of many women. But as it would be tedious to include all, consider some, and especially Deborah, whose virtue Scripture records for us.

44. For she showed not only that widows have no need of the help of a man, inasmuch as she, not at all restrained by the weakness of her sex, undertook to perform the duties of a man, and did even more than she had undertaken. And, at last, when the Jews were being ruled under the leadership of the judges, because they could not govern them with manly justice, or defend them with manly strength, and so wars broke out on all sides, they chose Deborah, by whose judgment they might be ruled. And so one widow both ruled many thousands of men in peace, and defended them from the enemy. There were many judges in Israel, but no woman before was a judge, as after Joshua there were many judges but none was a prophet. And I think that her judgeship has been narrated,

and her deeds described, that women should not be restrained from deeds of valor by the weakness of their sex. A widow, she governs the people; a widow, she leads armies; a widow, she chooses generals; a widow, she determines wars and orders triumphs. So, then, it is not nature which is answerable for the fault or which is liable to weakness. It is not sex, but valor which makes strong.

45. And in time of peace there is no complaint, and no fault is found in this woman whereas most of the judges were causes of no small sins to the people. But when the Canaanites, a people fierce in battle and rich in troops, successively joined them, showed a horrible disposition against the people of the Jews, this widow, before all others, made all the preparations for war. And to show that the needs of the household were not dependent on the public resources, but rather that public duties were guided by the discipline of home life, she brings forth from her home her son as leader of the army, that we may acknowledge that a widow can train a warrior; whom, as a mother, she taught, and, as judge, placed in command, as, being herself brave, she trained him, and, as a prophetess, sent to certain victory.

46. And lastly, her son Barak shows the chief part of the victory was in the hands of a woman when he said: "If thou wilt not go with me I will not go, for I know not the day on which the Lord sendeth His angel with me." How great, then, was the might of that woman to whom the leader of the army says, "If thou wilt not go I will not go." How great, I say, the fortitude of the widow who keeps not back her son from dangers through motherly affection, but rather with the zeal of a mother exhorts her

son to go forth to victory, while saying that the decisive point of that victory is in the hand of a woman!

47. So, then, Deborah foretold the event of the battle. Barak, as he was bidden, led forth the army; Jael carried off the triumph, for the prophecy of Deborah fought for her, who in a mystery revealed to us the rising of the Church from among the Gentiles, for whom should be found a triumph over Sisera, that is, over the powers opposed to her. For us, then, the oracles of the prophets fought, for us those judgments and arms of the prophets won the victory. And for this reason it was not the people of the Jews but Jael who gained the victory over the enemy. Unhappy, then, was that people which could not follow up by the virtue of faith the enemy, whom it had put to flight. And so by their fault salvation came to the Gentiles, by their sluggishness the victory was reserved for us.

48. Jael then destroyed Sisera, whom however the band of Jewish veterans had put to flight under their brilliant leader, for this is the interpretation of the name Barak; for often, as we read, the sayings and merits of the prophets procured heavenly aid for the fathers. But even at that time was victory being prepared over spiritual wickedness for those to whom it is said in the Gospel: "Come, ye blessed of My Father, take possession of the kingdom prepared for you from the foundation of the world." So the commencement of the victory was from the Fathers, its conclusion is in the Church.

49. But the Church does not overcome the powers of the enemy with weapons of this world, but with spiritual

arms, "which are mighty through God to the destruction of strongholds and the high places of spiritual wickedness." And Sisera's thirst was quenched with a bowl of milk, because he was overcome by wisdom, for what is healthful for us as food is deadly and weakening to the power of the enemy. The weapons of the Church are faith, the weapons of the Church are prayer, which overcomes the enemy.

50. And so according to this history a woman, that the minds of women might be stirred up, became a judge, a woman set all in order, a woman prophesied, a woman triumphed, and joining in the battle array taught men to war under a woman's lead. But in a mystery it is the battle of faith and the victory of the Church.

51. You, then, who are women have no excuse because of your nature. You who are widows have no excuse because of the weakness of your sex, nor can you attribute your changeableness to the loss of the support of a husband. Everyone has sufficient protection if courage is not wanting to the soul. And the very advance of age is a common defense of chastity for widows; and grief for the husband who is lost, regular work, the care of the house, anxiety for children, frequently ward off wantonness hurtful to the soul; while the very mourning attire, the funeral solemnities, the constant weeping, and grief impressed on the sad brow in deep wrinkles, restrains wanton eyes, checks lust, turns away forward looks. The sorrow of regretful affection is a good guardian of chastity, guilt cannot find an entrance if vigilance be not wanting.

CHAPTER IX.

To an objection that the state of widowhood might indeed be endurable if circumstances were pleasant, St. Ambrose replies that pleasant surroundings are more dangerous than even trouble; and goes to show by examples taken from holy Scripture, that widows may find much happiness in their children and their sons-in-law. They should have recourse to the Apostles, who are able to help us, and should entreat for the intercessions of angels and martyrs. He touches then on certain complaints respecting loneliness, and care of property, and ends by pointing out the unseemliness of a widow marrying who has daughters either married already or of marriageable age.

52. You have learnt, then, you who are widows, that you are not destitute of the help of nature, and that you can maintain sound counsel. Nor, again, are you devoid of protection at home, who are able to claim even the highest point of public power.

53. But perhaps someone may say that widowhood is more endurable for her who enjoys prosperity, but that widows are soon broken down by adversity, and easily succumb. On which point not only are we taught by experience that enjoyment is more perilous for widows than difficulties, but by the examples in the Scriptures that even in weakness widows are not usually without aid, and that divine and human support is furnished more readily to them than to others, if they have brought up children and chosen sons-in-law well. And, finally, when Simon's mother-in-law was lying sick with violent fever, Peter and Andrew besought the Lord for her: "And He stood over her and commanded the fever and it left her, and immediately she arose and ministered unto them."

54. "She was taken," it is said, "with a great fever, and they besought him for her." You too have those near you to entreat for you. You have the Apostles near, you have the Martyrs near; if associated with the Martyrs in devotion, you draw near them also by works of mercy. Do you show mercy and you will be close to Peter. It is not relationship by blood but affinity of virtue which makes near, for we walk not in the flesh but in the Spirit. Cherish, then, the nearness of Peter and the affinity of Andrew, that they may pray for you and your lusts give way. Touched by the word of God you, who lay on the earth, will then forthwith rise up to minister to Christ. "For our conversation is in heaven, whence also we look for the Savior, the Lord Jesus Christ." For no one lying down can minister to Christ. Minister to the poor and you have ministered to Christ. "For what ye have done unto one of these," He says, "ye have done unto Me." You, widows, have then assistance, if you choose such sons-in-law for yourselves, such patrons and friends for your posterity.

55. So Peter and Andrew prayed for the widow. Would that there were some one who could so quickly pray for us, or better still, they who prayed for the mother-in-law, Peter and Andrew his brother. Then they could pray for one related to them, now they are able to pray for us and for all. For you see that one bound by great sin is less fit to pray for herself, certainly less likely to obtain for herself. Let her then make use of others to pray for her to the physician. For the sick, unless the physician be called to them by the prayers of others, cannot pray for themselves. The flesh is weak, the soul is sick and hindered by the chains of sins, and cannot direct its feeble

steps to the throne of that physician. The angels must be entreated for us, who have been to us as guards; the martyrs must be entreated, whose patronage we seem to claim for ourselves by the pledge as it were of their bodily remains. They can entreat for our sins, who, if they had any sins, washed them in their own blood; for they are the martyrs of God, our leaders, the beholders of our life and of our actions. Let us not be ashamed to take them as intercessors for our weakness, for they themselves knew the weaknesses of the body, even when they overcame.

56. So, then, Peter's mother-in-law found some to pray for her. And you, O widow, find those who will pray for you, if as a true widow and desolate you hope in God, continue instant in supplications, persist in prayers, treat your body as dying daily, that by dying you may live again; avoid pleasures, that you, too, being sick, may be healed. "For she that liveth in pleasure is dead while she liveth."

57. You have no longer any reason for marrying, you have some to intercede for you. Say not, "I am desolate." This is the complaint of one who wishes to marry. Say not, "I am alone." Chastity seeks solitude: the modest seek privacy, the immodest company. But you have necessary business; you have also one to plead for you. You are afraid of your adversary; the Lord Himself will intervene with the judge and say: "Judge for the fatherless, and justify the widow."

58. But you wish to take care of your inheritance. The inheritance of modesty is greater, and this a widow can guard better than one married. A slave has done wrong.

Forgive him, for it is better that you should bear with another's fault than expose it. But you wish to marry. Be it so. The simple desire is no crime. I do not ask the reason, why is one invented? If you think it good, say so; if unsuitable, be silent. Do not blame God, do not blame your relatives, saying that protection fails you. Would that the wish did not fail! And say not that you are consulting the interests of your children, whom you are depriving of their mother.

59. There are some things permissible in the abstract, but not permissible on account of age. Why is the bridal of the mother being prepared at the same time with that of the daughters, and often even afterwards? Why does the grown-up daughter learn to blush in the presence of her mother's betrothed rather than her own? I confess that I advised you to change your dress, but not to put on a bridal veil; to go away from the tomb, not to prepare a bridal couch. What is the meaning of a newly-married woman who already has sons-in-law? How unseemly it is to have children younger than one's grand-children!

CHAPTER X.

St. Ambrose returns again to the subject of Christ, speaking of His goodness in all misery. The various ways in which the good Physician treats our diseases, and the quickness of the healing if only we do not neglect to call upon Him. He touches upon the moral meaning of the will, which he shows was manifested in Peter's mother-in-law, and lastly points out what a minister of Christ and specially a bishop ought to be, and says that they specially must rise through grace.

60. BUT let us return to the point, and not, while we are grieving over the wounds of our sins, leave the physician, and whilst ministering to the sores of others, let our own go on increasing. The Physician is then here asked for. Do not fear, because the Lord is great, that perhaps He will not condescend to come to one who is sick, for He often comes to us from heaven; and is wont to visit not only the rich but also the poor and the servants of the poor. And so now He comes, when called upon, to Peter's mother-in-law. "And He stood over her and rebuked the fever, and it left her, and immediately she arose and ministered unto them." As He is worthy of being remembered, so, too, is He worthy of being longed for, worthy, too, of love, for His condescension to every single matter which affects men, and His marvelous acts. He disdains not to visit widows, and to enter the narrow rooms of a poor cottage. As God He commands, as man He visits.

61. Thanks be to the Gospel, by means of which we also, who saw not Christ when He came into this world, seem to be with Him when we read His deeds, that as they, to whom He drew near, borrowed faith from Him, so may He, when we believe His deeds, draw near to us.

62. Do you see what kinds of healing are with Him? He commands the fever, He commands the unclean spirits, at another place He lays hands on them. He was wont then to heal the sick, not only by word but also by touch. And do you then, who burn with many desires, taken either by the beauty or by the fortune of someone, implore Christ, call in the Physician, stretch forth your right hand to Him, let the hand of God touch your inmost being, and the grace of the heavenly Word enter the veins of your inward desires, let God's right hand strike the secrets of your heart. He spreads clay on the eyes of some that they may see, and the Creator of all teaches us that we ought to be mindful of our own nature, and to discern the vileness of our body; for no one can see divine things except one who through knowledge of his vileness cannot be puffed up. Another is bidden to show himself to the priest, that he may for ever be free from the scales of leprosy. For he alone can preserve his purity, both of body and soul, who knows how to show himself to that priest, Whom we have received as an Advocate for our sins, and to Whom is plainly said: "Thou art a priest for ever after the order of Melchisedech."

63. And be not afraid that there will be any delay in healing. He who is healed by Christ has no hindrances. You must use the remedy which you have received; and as soon as He has given the command, the blind man sees, the paralytic walks, the dumb speaks, the deaf hears, she that has a fever ministers, the lunatic is delivered. And do you, then, whoever after an unseemly fashion languish for desire of anything, entreat the Lord, show Him your faith, and fear no delay. Where there is prayer, the Word is present, desire is put to flight, lust departs. And be not

afraid of offending by confession, take it rather as a right, for you who were before afflicted by an intense disease of the body will begin to minister to Christ.

64. And in this place can be seen the disposition of the will of Peter's mother-in-law, from which she received for herself, as it were, the seed corn of what was to come, for to each his will is the cause of that which is to come. For from the will springs wisdom, which the wise man takes in marriage to himself, saying: "I desire to make her my spouse." This will, then, which at first was weak and languid under the fever of various desires, afterwards by the office of the apostles rose up strong to minister unto Christ.

65. At the same time it is also shown what he ought to be who ministers to Christ, for first he must be free from the enticements of various pleasures, he must be free from inward languor of body and soul, that he may minister the Body and Blood of Christ. For no one who is sick with his own sins, and far from being whole, can minister the remedies of the healing of immortality. See what thou doest, O priest, and touch not the Body of Christ with a fevered hand. First be healed that thou mayest be able to minister. If Christ bids those who are now cleansed, but were once leprous, to show themselves to the priests, how much more is it fitting for the priest himself to be pure. That widow, then, cannot take it ill that I have not spared her, since I spare not myself.

66. Peter's mother-in-law, it is written, rose up and ministered to them. Well is it said, rose up, for the grace of the apostleship was already furnishing a type of the

sacrament. It is proper to the ministers of Christ to rise, according to that which is written: "Awake, thou that sleepest, and arise from the dead."

CHAPTER XI.

Having shown that the pretexts usually alleged for second marriages have no weight, St. Ambrose declares that he does not condemn them, though from the Apostle's words he sets forth their inconveniences, though the state of those twice married is approved in the Church, and he takes occasion to advert to those heretics who forbid them. And he says that it is because the strength of different persons varies that chastity is not commanded, but only recommended.

67. I SAY, then, that widows who have been in the habit of giving neither are in want of their necessary expenses, nor of help, who in very great dangers have often guarded the resources of their husbands; and further, I think that the good offices of a husband are usually made up for to them by sons-in-law and other relatives, and that God's mercy is more ready to help them, and therefore, when there is no special cause for marrying, the desire of so doing should not exist.

68. This, however, I say as a counsel, we do not order it as a precept, stirring up the wills of widows rather than binding them. For I do not forbid second marriages, only I do not advise them. The consideration of human weakness is one thing, the grace of chastity is another. I say more, I do not forbid second, but do not approve of often repeated marriages, for not everything is expedient which is lawful: "All things are lawful to me," says the Apostle, "but all things are not expedient." As, also, to drink wine is lawful, but, for the most part, it is not expedient.

69. It is then lawful to marry, but it is more seemly to abstain, for there are bonds in marriage. Do you ask what bonds? "The woman who is under a husband is bound by

the law so long as her husband liveth; but if her husband be dead she is loosed from the law of her husband." It is then proved that marriage is a bond by which the woman is bound and from which she is loosed. Beautiful is the grace of mutual love, but the bondage is more constant. "The wife hath not power of her own body, but the husband." And lest this bondage should seem to be rather one of sex than of marriage, there follows: "Likewise, also, the husband hath not power of his own body, but the wife." How great; then, is the constraint in marriage, which subjects even the stronger to the other; for by mutual constraint each is bound to serve. Nor if one wishes to refrain can he withdraw his neck from the yoke, for he is subject to the incontinence of the other. It is said: "Ye are bought with a price, be not ye servants of men." You see how plainly the servitude of marriage is defined. It is not I who say this, but the Apostle; or, rather, it is not he, but Christ, Who spoke in him. And he spoke of this servitude in the case of good married people. For above you read: "The unbelieving husband is sanctified by his believing wife; and the unbelieving wife by her believing husband." And further on: "But if the unbelieving depart, let him depart. A brother or a sister is not bound in such cases." If, then, a good marriage is servitude, what is a bad one, when they cannot sanctify, but destroy one another?

70. But as I exhort widows to keep the grace of their gift, so, too, I incite women to observe ecclesiastical discipline, for the Church is made up of all. Though it be the flock of Christ, yet some are fed on strong food, others are still nourished with milk, who must be on their guard against those wolves who are hidden in sheep's

clothing, pretending to all appearance of continence, but inciting to the foulness of incontinence. For they know how severe are the burdens of chastity, since they cannot touch them with the tips of their fingers; they require of others that which is above measure, when they themselves cannot even observe any measure, but rather give way under the cruel weight. For the measure of the burden must always be according to the strength of him who has to bear it; otherwise, where the bearer is weak, he breaks down with the burden laid upon him; for too strong meat chokes the throats of infants.

71. And so as in a multitude of bearers their strength is not estimated by that of a few; nor do the stronger receive their tasks in accordance with the weakness of others, but each is allowed to bear as great a burden as he desires, the reward increasing with the increase of strength; so, too, a snare is not to be set for women, nor a burden of continence beyond their strength to be taken up, but it must be left to each to weigh the matter for herself, not compelled by the authority of any command, but incited by increase of grace. And so for different degrees of virtue a different reward is set forth, and one thing is not blamed that another may be praised; but all are spoken of, in order that what is best may be preferred.

CHAPTER XII.

The difference between matters of precept and of counsel is treated of, as shown in the case of the young man in the Gospel, and the difference of the rewards set forth both for counsels and precepts is spoken of.

72. MARRIAGE, then, is honorable, but chastity is more honorable, for "he that giveth his virgin in marriage doeth well, but he that giveth her not in marriage doeth better." That, then, which is good need not be avoided, but that which is better should be chosen. And so it is not laid upon any, but set before him. And, therefore, the Apostle said well: "Concerning virgins I have no commandment of the Lord, yet I give my counsel." For a command is issued to those subject, counsel is given to friends. Where there is a commandment, there is a law; where counsel, there is grace. A commandment is given to enforce what is according to nature, a counsel to incite us to follow grace. And, therefore, the Law was given to the Jews, but grace was reserved for the elect. The Law was given that, through fear of punishment, it might recall those who were wandering beyond the limits of nature, to their observance, but grace to incite the elect both by the desire of good things, and also by the promised rewards.

73. You will see the difference between precept and counsel, if you remember the case of him in the Gospel, to whom it is first commanded to do no murder, not to commit adultery, not to bear false witness; for that is a commandment which has a penalty for its transgression. But when he said that he had fulfilled all the commandments of the Law, there is given to him a counsel that he should sell all that he had and follow the

Lord, for these things are not imposed as commands, but are offered as counsels. For there are two ways of commanding things, one by way of precept, the other by way of counsel. And so the Lord in one way says: "Thou shalt not kill," where He gives a commandment; in the other He says: "If thou wilt be perfect, sell all that thou hast." He is, then, not bound by a commandment to whom the choice is left.

74. And so they who have fulfilled the commandments are able to say: "We are unprofitable servants, we have done that which was our duty to do." The virgin does not say this, nor he who sold all his goods, but they rather await the stored-up rewards like the holy Apostle who says: "Behold we have forsaken all and followed Thee, what shall we have therefore?" He says not, like the unprofitable servant, that he has done that which was his duty to do, but as being profitable to his Master, because he has multiplied the talents entrusted to him by the increase he has gained, having a good conscience, and without anxiety as to his merits he expects the reward of his faith and virtue. And so it is said to him and the others: "Ye which have followed Me, in the regeneration, when the Son of Man shall sit in the throne of His glory, shall also yourselves sit upon twelve thrones, judging the tribes of Israel." And to those who had faithfully preserved their talents He promises rewards indeed, though smaller saying: "Because thou hast been faithful over a few things, I will make thee ruler over many things." Good faith, then, is due, but mercy is in the rewards. He who has kept good faith has deserved that good faith should be kept with him; he who has made

good profit, because he has not sought his own benefit, has gained a claim to a heavenly reward.

CHAPTER XIII.

St. Ambrose, treating of the words in the Gospel concerning eunuchs, condemns those who make themselves such. Those only deserve praise who have through continence gained the victory over themselves, but no one is to be compelled to live this life, as neither Christ nor the Apostle laid down such a law, so that the marriage vow is not to be blamed, though that of chastity is better.

75. So, then, a commandment to this effect is not given, but a counsel is. Chastity is commanded, entire continence counseled. "But all men cannot receive this saying, but they to whom it is given. For there are eunuchs which were so born from their mother's womb," in whom exists a natural necessity not the virtue of chastity. "And there are eunuchs who have made themselves eunuchs," of their own will, that is, not of necessity. "And there are eunuchs which were made eunuchs of men..." And, therefore, great is the grace of continence in them, because it is the will, not incapacity, which makes a man continent. For it is seemly to preserve the gift of divine working whole. And let them not think it too little not to be impeded by the inclination of the body, for if the reward for going through that conflict is taken from their reach, the matter of sin is also removed, and though they cannot receive the crown, no more can they be overcome. They have other kinds of virtues by which they ought to commend themselves if their faith be firm, their mercifulness abundant, avarice far from them, grace abundant. But in them there is no fault, for they are ignorant of the act of sin.

76. The case is not the same of those who mutilate themselves, and I touch upon this point advisedly, for

there are some who look upon it as a holy deed to check by the evil violence of this sort. And though I am not willing to express my own opinion concerning them, though decisions of our forefathers are in existence; but then consider whether this tends not rather to a declaration of weakness than to a reputation for strength. On this principle no one should fight lest he be overcome, nor make use of his feet, fearing the danger of stumbling, nor let his eyes do their office because he fears a fall through lust. But what does it profit to cut the flesh, when there may be guilt even in a look? "For whosoever looketh on a woman to lust after her hath committed adultery already with her in his heart." And likewise she who looks on a man to lust after him commits adultery. It becomes us, then, to be chaste, not weak, to have our eyes modest, not feeble.

77. No one, then, ought, as many suppose, to mutilate himself, but rather gain the victory; for the Church gathers in those who conquer, not those who are defeated. And why should I use arguments when the words of the Apostle's command are at hand? For you find it thus written: "I would that they were mutilated who desire that you should be circumcised." For why should the means of gaining a crown and of the practice of virtue be lost to a man who is born to honor, equipped for victory? how can he through courage of soul mutilate himself? "There be eunuchs which have made themselves eunuchs for the kingdom of heaven's sake."

78. This, however, is not a commandment given to all, but a wish set before all. For he who commands must always keep to the exact scope of the commandments, and he

who distributes tasks must observe equity in looking into them, for: "A false balance is abomination to the Lord." There is, then, an excess and a defect in weight, but the Church accepts neither, for: "Excessive and defective weights and divers measures, both of them are alike abominable in the sight of the Lord." There are tasks which wisdom apportions, and apportions according to the estimate of the virtue and strength of each. "He that is able to receive it let him receive it."

79. For the Creator of all knows that the dispositions of each are different, and therefore incited virtue by rewards, instead of binding weakness by chains. And he, the teacher of the Gentiles, the good guide of our conduct, and instructor of our inmost affections, who had learnt in himself that the law of the flesh resists the law of the mind, but yields to the grace of Christ, he knows, I say, that various movements of the mind are opposed to each other; and, therefore, so expresses his exhortations to chastity, as not to do away with the grace of marriage, nor has he so exalted marriage as to check the desire of chastity. But beginning with the recommendation of chastity, he goes on to remedies against incontinence, and having set before the stronger the prize of their high calling, he suffers no one to faint by the way; approving those who take the lead so as not to make little of those who follow. For he, himself, had learnt that the Lord Jesus gave to some barley bread lest they should faint by the way, and administered His Body to others, that they might strive for the kingdom.

80. For the Lord Himself did not impose this commandment, but invited the will, and the Apostle did

not lay down a rule, but gave a counsel. But this not a man's counsel as to things within the compass of man's strength, for he acknowledges that the gift of divine mercy was bestowed upon him, that he might know how faithfully to set first the former, and to arrange the latter. And, therefore, he says: "I think," not, I order, but, "I think that this is good because of the present distress."

81. The marriage bond is not then to be shunned as though it were sinful, but rather declined as being a galling burden. For the law binds the wife to bear children in labor and in sorrow, and is in subjection to her husband, for that he is lord over her. So, then, the married woman, but not the widow, is subject to labor and pain in bringing forth children, and she only that is married, not she that is a virgin, is under the power of her husband. The virgin is free from all these things, who has vowed her affection to the Word of God, who awaits the Spouse of blessing with her lamp burning with the light of a good will. And so she is moved by counsels, not bound by chains.

CHAPTER XIV.

Though a widow may have received no commandment, yet she has received so many counsels that she ought not to think little of them. St. Ambrose would be sorry to lay any snare for her, seeing that the field of the Church grows richer as a result of wedlock, but it is absolutely impossible to deny that widowhood, which St. Paul praises, is profitable. Consequently, he speaks severely about those who have proscribed widowhood by law.

82. But neither has the widow received any command, but a counsel; a counsel, however, not given once only but often repeated. For, first, it is said: "It is good for a man not to touch a woman." And again: "I would that all men were even as I myself;" and once more: "It is good for them if they remain even as I;" and a fourth time: "It is good for the present distress." And that it is well pleasing to the Lord, and honorable, and, lastly, that perseverance in widowhood is happier, he lays down not only as his own judgment, but also as an aspiration of the Holy Spirit. Who, then, can reject the kindness of such a counselor? Who gives the reins to the will, and advises in the case of others that which he has found advantageous by his own experience, he who is not easy to catch up, and is not hurt at being equaled. Who, then, would shrink from becoming holy in body and spirit, since the reward is far above the toil, grace beyond need, and the wages above the work?

83. And this, I say, not in order to lay a snare for others, but that as a good husbandman of the land entrusted to me, I may see this field of the Church to be fruitful, at one time blossoming with the flowers of purity, at another time strong in the gravity of widowhood, and yet again abounding with the fruits of wedlock. For though they be diverse, yet they are the fruits of one field; there are not

so many lilies in the gardens as ears of corn in the fields, and many more fields are prepared for receiving seed than lie fallow after the crops are gathered in.

84. Widowhood is, then, good, which is so often praised by the judgment of the apostles, for it is a teacher of the faith and a teacher of chastity. Whereas they who honor the adulteries and the shame of their gods appointed penalties for celibacy and widowhood; that zealous in pursuit of crimes they might punish the study of virtues; under the pretext, indeed, of seeking increase of the population, but in reality that they might put an end to the purpose of chastity. For the soldier, when his time is ended, lays aside his arms, and leaving the rank which he held, is dismissed as a veteran to his own land, that he may obtain rest after the toils of a laborious life, and cause others to be more ready to undergo labor in the hope of future repose. The laborer, too, as he grows too old, entrusts the guiding of the plough to others, and worn out by the toil of his youth, enjoys in his old age that which his foresight has cared for, still ready to prune the vine rather than to press the grapes, so as to check the luxuriance of early life, and to cut off with his pruning knife the wantonness of youth, teaching, as it were, that blessed fruitfulness is to be aimed at even in the vine.

85. In like manner the widow, as a veteran, having served her time, though she lays aside the arms of married life, yet orders the peace of the whole house: though now freed from carrying burdens, she is yet watchful for the younger who are to be married; and with the thoughtfulness of old age she arranges where more pains would be profitable, where produce would be more abundant, which is fitted

for the marriage bond. And so, if the field is entrusted to the elder rather than to the younger, why should you think that it is more advantageous to be a married woman than a widow? But, if the persecutors of the faith have also been the persecutors of widowhood, most certainly by those who hold the faith, widowhood is not to be shunned as a penalty, but to be esteemed as a reward.

CHAPTER XV.

St. Ambrose meets the objection of those who make the desire of having children an excuse for second marriage, and especially in the case of those who have children of their former marriage; and points out the consequent troubles of disagreements amongst the children, and even between the married persons, and gives a warning against a wrong use of Scripture instances in this matter.

86. PERHAPS, however, it may seem good to some that marriage should again be entered upon for the sake of having children. But if the desire of children be a reason for marrying, certainly where there are children, the reason does not exist. And is it wise to wish to have a second trial of that fruitfulness which has already been tried in vain, or to submit to the solitude which you have already borne? This is the case of those who have no children.

87. Then, too, she who has borne children, and has lost them (for she who has a hope of bearing children will have an intenser longing), does not she, I say, seem to herself to be covering over the deaths of her lost children by the celebration of a second marriage? Will she not again suffer what she is again seeking? and does she not shrink at the graves of her hopes, the memories of the bereavements she has suffered, the voices of the mourners? Or, when the torches are lit and night is coming on, does she not think rather that funeral rites are being prepared than a bridal chamber? Why, then, my daughter, do you seek again those sorrows which you dread, more than you look for children whom you no longer hope for? If sorrow is so grievous, one should rather avoid than seek that which causes it.

88. And what advice shall I give to you who have children? What reason have you for marrying? Perhaps foolish light-mindedness, or the habit of incontinence, or the consciousness of a wounded spirit is urging you on. But counsel is given to the sober, not to the drunken, and so my words are addressed to the free conscience which is whole in each respect. She that is wounded has a remedy, she that is upright a counsel. What do you intend to do then, my daughter? Why do you seek for heirs from without when you have your own? You are not desiring of children, for you have them, but servitude from which you are free. For this true servitude, in which love is exhausted, which no longer the charm of virginity, and early youth, full of holy modesty and grace, excites; when offences are more felt, and rudeness is more suspected, and agreement less common, which is not bound fast by love deeply rooted by time, or by beauty in its prime of youth. Duty to a husband is burdensome, so that you are afraid to love your children and blush to look at them; and a cause of disagreement arises from that which ordinarily causes mutual love to increase the tender affections of parents. You wish to give birth to offspring who will be not the brothers but the adversaries of your children. For what is to bring forth other children other than to rob the children which you have, who are deprived alike of the offices of affection and of the profit of their possessions.

89. The divine law has bound together husband and wife by its authority, and yet mutual love remains a difficult matter. For God took a rib from the man, and formed the woman so as to join them one to the other, and said: "They shall be one flesh." He said this not of a second marriage but of the first, for neither did Eve take a second

husband, nor does holy Church recognize a second bridegroom. "For that is a great mystery in Christ and in the Church. Neither, again, did Isaac know another wife besides Rebecca, nor bury his father, Abraham, with any wife but Sarah."

90. But in holy Rachel[3408] there was rather the figure of a mystery than a true order of marriage. Notwithstanding, in her, also, we have something which we can refer to the grace of the first marriage, since he loved her best whom he had first betrothed, and deceit did not shut out his intention, nor the intervening marriage destroy his love for his betrothed. And so the holy patriarch has taught us, how highly we ought to esteem a first marriage, since he himself esteemed his first betrothal so highly. Take care, then, my daughter, lest you be both unable to hold fast the grace of marriage, and also increase your own troubles.

www.ingramcontent.com/pod-product-compliance
Lightning Source LLC
Chambersburg PA
CBHW052119070526
44584CB00017B/2552